LOVING
GRIEF

LOVING GRIEF

Paul Bennett

LARSON PUBLICATIONS
Burdett, New York

ISBN-10: 0-943914-64-7
ISBN-13: 978-0-943914-64-0

Library of Congress Control Number: 2009925305

Publisher's Cataloging-In-Publication Data
(Prepared by The Donohue Group, Inc.)

Bennett, Paul (Paul S.)
  Loving grief / Paul Bennett.

  p. ; cm.

  ISBN-13: 978-0-943914-64-0
  ISBN-10: 0-943914-64-7

1. Grief. 2. Bereavement--Psychological aspects. 3. Loss (Psychology)
4. Widowhood--Psychological aspects. 5. Widowers. 6. Adjustment
(Psychology) I. Title.

BF575.G7 B46 2009
155.9/37   2009925305

Published by Larson Publications
4936 NYS Route 414
Burdett, New York 14818 USA

larsonpublications.com

18 17 16 15 14 13 12 11 10 09
    10 9 8 7 6 5 4 3 2 1

Contents

The Beginning and the End

          DEEP in the night of Friday, December 13th, 2002, Bonnie woke up. I asked her if anything was wrong.

"I feel totally miserable."

"Is something hurting you?"

"No."

"Are you nauseous?"

"No. I'm completely miserable. I want to stop taking the medicine. I don't want this to go on anymore."

This was twenty-three years after the summer we fell in love. We had been married for twenty years. For the last two years, Bonnie had been treated for cancer. For ten weeks, we had known that a tumor was growing in her brain, and there was nothing we could do to stop it.

This night, Bonnie was telling me she was ready to die.

This was the last conversation of our lives. It wasn't

much, and it was everything: She said she was only afraid of being in terrible pain if she stopped taking the steroids that were controlling the swelling of her brain.

I told her I believed we were ready to control the pain. I promised to call the hospice nurse and the oncologist in the morning and make sure we were ready. Eager to have her free from worrying, I urged her to go back to sleep. She did. I did.

The next day, Bonnie could speak only enough to ask for water or for help to the bathroom. Sunday, there wasn't even that. On Tuesday morning, with her daughter, her sister and me sitting beside her, holding her, stroking her, she died.

This book is what I would say softly to you if you and I were sitting on the porch after the setting sun has left us, two shadows facing each other . . . or if perhaps your head rested on my shoulder as your tears ran . . . this book is what I would murmur to you about grief.

Knowing Grief

I KNOW a little about grief, about my grief. I was fortunate to see early on that my grief is my own, not measured or predicted by anyone else's. It need not look like anyone else's grief, any more than my love for Bonnie needed to look like anyone else's love.

Still, people see reflections of ourselves in others. We recognize glimmers of our own love in other people's love. I hear echoes of my grief in other people's grief. And some of the many things people said and wrote to me about grief did give me a clearer view of what was happening in me, did help me to go through those sad days more peacefully, did help me make peace with Bonnie's death.

So I offer these reflections for anyone who is grieving or who loves someone who's grieving. *They are as true as I can write them, but they are not the only truth about grief.*

Fundamentally, what I'm writing about is love. Early on, I took comfort in the knowledge that grief is the way my love for Bonnie feels. What I was feeling when I felt so bad was my love for her. What I was feeling on brighter days, too, was my love for her.

I took heart from my confidence that grief changes, just like love does. The way I loved Bonnie after twenty years of marriage was not the way I loved her when we first fell in love. My grief two years after she died is not the same as the grief I experienced in the first weeks and months. Just as my love felt different from day to day while Bonnie was with me, so my grief feels different from day to day and month to month now that she is lost.

I began this book about a year after Bonnie died. By then my life and my grief were vastly different from what they had been, and they continue to change as I write. Through all the change, though, there is something permanent in my grief for Bonnie, because there is something permanent in my love for her. At her memorial service I described that permanence as "Bonnie's canyon." My progress through grief has been progress in discovering the shape of my love for Bonnie, even as it changes.

These reflections are written in small pieces. I don't want to impose an organization that was absent from the experience itself. I felt disoriented much of the time, and what I held onto were very small things, like the short pieces of poetry or prose I have put at the end of each chapter.

What follows here is a story of discovery. In grief I discovered a life within me that includes and embraces Bonnie.

While careening down through the tumultuous feelings that followed her death, I found that there was growth, and there was a destination. Every day, I can look at where I am and say, "I am here because I loved Bonnie. Because she loved me. And because she died."

Where do I go now?
What is my task?
Am I to heal?
Can a scar cover
The lack of you?
Am I to move on?
I've lost the knack
Of locomotion.
What now? Where now?
Who shall I be
Now that I can't be yours?

Speaking Grief

ALMOST as soon as Bonnie died, I began trying to express my grief in words. I'm comfortable with words; what's written down seems more stable, more approachable, available to contemplation. So I began to talk and to write about my grief as soon as I knew it had begun. Two of the people I spoke to (my friend Susan Bachurski and Gretchen Gaines, a grief counselor) suggested I write about this for others.

Each opportunity I had to share my love for Bonnie with others was precious, because mostly I did my grieving alone. My daughter, Rebecca, was living with me, and we spoke about Bonnie, scattered her ashes together, reminisced about her beauty and her love . . . but grief is a twenty-four-hour phenomenon, so grief is fundamentally something you do alone.

The wisest of friends know that grief is not something

that can be fixed or needs to be fixed. The wisest of friends know that grief is something that we must pass through; it is the way love feels now, and not the way love will always feel. And when the grieving person speaks, the greatest and most healing gift is listening. Since then I've learned that in any conversation, the quality of listening is just as important as the quality of speaking. It was into a deep listening that I spoke at Bonnie's memorial service a few days after she died, the memorial service she had designed.

This week we've spent time looking at pictures of Bonnie, something she really didn't like to do. She would wrinkle her nose at them and flip quickly past the pictures of herself. And she was right.

Because pictures of Bonnie never did her justice.

Photographs are too still to hold the liveliness of her smile.

Pigments are too harsh or too dull to render the warmth that was pooled deep in her eyes.

Still, I always wanted those pictures. Near my desk is a picture of Bonnie that I took twenty-three years ago, when we were first discovering our love for each other. She was snuggled in a blanket, in front of a fire; if you look closely in the darks of her eyes, you can see tiny reflections of the flames. It was an accident, a trick of the lens—you might say a photographic metaphor.

But only metaphor can catch her magic.

Last May, on the coast of Italy, she walked up a famous footpath out of the town of Monterosso, up through the vineyards, breathlessly up five hundred and seventy-three ancient stone steps. (Yes, later she walked them again and counted each one.) At the top, on the heights overlooking the Mediterranean, she begged me, Let's go on to the next town, though it was an hour away or more, though we had flown across the Atlantic that day and the sun was already setting. She was ready to risk being caught in the dark on a rocky, winding path hundreds of feet above the sea . . . just to discover, as soon as possible, a beauty that she had not yet known.

I picture Bonnie in high places. I picture her in the bell tower of San Giorgio Maggiore, also last spring, looking across the Venetian lagoon toward Piazza San Marco, drinking in that spectacular vista, but already impatient to go down and venture more deeply into the history and architecture and art of Venice.

I picture her hiking up toward the top of the canyon in Chiricahua National Monument in eastern Arizona. We hiked all afternoon, up into an improbable landscape: huge towers of balanced rocks created by an ancient volcanic upheaval, a landscape that seemed to have waited millions of years just for her to discover it.

But pictures of Bonnie never did her justice. And if I have one fear about living without her, it's this—that the pictures I hold in my memory and my heart may not, in the end, do justice to her life, and her love.

Only metaphor can catch her magic.

Bonnie loved to walk by water, through nature nourished, brightened and soothed by a river or stream. So we often found ourselves in canyons, where water not only nourishes life but has shaped the earth itself.

Even when a river stops flowing, the canyon remains, an emptiness, a vast emptiness but endowed with permanent beauty that the flow of the river has carved.

I am Bonnie's canyon. For twenty-three years the gentle but irresistible flow of her life has filled me up, opened me, and stroked my ragged edges smooth. Whatever is sinuous or gentle in the rock of me has taken its shape from her overflowing grace.

IN THOSE DAYS I did feel like rock, dry and immobile. I felt empty. It's amazing that such an overflow of feeling can seem so much like the absence of any feeling whatsoever. But the immobility was an illusion. Actually, my grief was changing constantly.

More than a month later, Bonnie's colleagues at the National Rehabilitation Hospital, many of whom had not been able to attend her memorial service just before Christmas, held a memorial service of their own following the model that Bonnie had given us. In the course of that month, I had moved from concentrating on the emptiness of Bonnie's absence to grappling with my sense of her presence. Here's some of what I said to those people who had just given me a precious vision of Bonnie as a therapist and a colleague.

> You've talked about what Bonnie gave you. But don't forget what delight you gave her.
>
> She was hungry for life, and your lives fed her. She thirsted for friendship and love, and from you she drank deep.
>
> In January of 2001, Bonnie and I attended a concert, a sort of anti-inauguration with others who weren't pleased with the election. There were speakers as well as music, and one preacher told us to turn and look at the person next to us.
>
> "You are sitting next to a miracle," he said.

I looked at Bonnie and thought, "This preacher knows what he's talking about."

Then he said, "The miracle next to you is going through hell, or has gone through hell, or is about to go through hell."

Remarkably, I did not think about his words a few days later, when Bonnie, my personal miracle, was diagnosed with a rare and dangerous melanoma.

But I did think about it after Bonnie died, and on reflection I realized that that preacher was utterly, profoundly . . . wrong.

Bonnie would not let her life be hell.

Instead, she proceeded to enchant every surgeon and oncologist, every nurse and phlebotomist and X-ray tech she met. She knew she was in danger, but she knew that good days were there for her to take. They had to be earned with days of treatment, days of weariness, with drug injections and blood draws, endless needle sticks.

But if the cost of her good days had gone up, it made them, if anything, more precious.

Time after time she bounced back to return to a job that inspired her. She bounced back to travel to Michigan and Italy, and to take part in her sister's wedding, and most of all to live her own life, day by day.

Bonnie took all those good days. And then, when she knew there were no good days left, she accepted that without fear; she decided not to prolong her life. She asked only to be surrounded by those she loved and to be free of pain. And she quietly slipped away over the next three days.

I want to tell you this. When Bonnie died, her face, which had been placid and serene through those last days . . . her face took on a small, Buddha's smile. It was the smile, it seemed to me, of someone who was at peace with her life, at peace with her death, because she had done both so perfectly well.

She had asked us to look for something we found only after her death, a passage by Emily Carr:

"There is nothing as strong as growing. Nothing can drown that force that splits rocks and pavements and spreads over the fields. Man can pattern it and change its variety and shape, but leave it for even a short time and off it goes, swamping and swallowing man's puny intentions. No killing or stamping down can destroy it. Life is in the soil. Touch it with air and light and it bursts forth like a struck match. Nothing is dead, not even a corpse. It moves into the elements when the spirit has left it, but even to the spirit's leaving there is life, boundless life, resistless and marvelous, fresh and clean."

I think it's not only into nature that Bonnie returns, it's also into us.

I think that when Bonnie was alive, we were too dazzled by her physical warmth to see how far her miracle reached into us—just as scientists can study the corona that surrounds the sun only when the sun itself is eclipsed.

With the shadow of mourning settled over us, our eyes grow more sensitive, and we can see the miracle of Bonnie that glows in each of us.

I'm talking about more than memories. Each of us, in our way, has learned to see with Bonnie's eyes and to listen with Bonnie's heart. We all have some piece of her miracle, and when we come together, it multiplies. Together, we hold in us the miracle that is Bonnie.

Hold her tight.
Hold her tight.

AT THE TIME of this second memorial service, about six weeks after Bonnie died, I was early in my grief; living without Bonnie would become much, much harder before it began to be easier. But already, my view of Bonnie's legacy to me had changed. I had come to see that what Bonnie had left within me was not a fixed shape carved out of my lifelessness, but a way of living and growing.

The passage by Emily Carr had reminded Bonnie that she believed in the power of life. Later, even as she contemplated her own death and planned the memorial service that she would ask us to create for her, it was life she focused on, not death. Her belief in the power of life comforted me and inspired me to believe in life in a way I never had before.

Today, reading what I said that January, I hear myself struggling with the contradiction between my belief and my experience, between the comfort of my belief in life and the utter inconsolability of my feelings. I was struggling to understand how I could believe in Emily Carr's unstoppable power of life and yet feel no strength to live my own life. For months, I would struggle to reconcile the contradiction between my conviction of Bonnie's living presence within me and my overwhelming loneliness at her absence.

> *Grief has pulled me open,*
> *And I see that the life within me*
> *will always embrace you.*
> *And in that life is growth,*
> *toward a destination I cannot imagine.*

A Brief Life

I DIDN'T set out to write a life of Bonnie, but how can I talk about losing her without telling you a little bit about who she was? When she first came into my life—or rather when she changed from a casual business acquaintance to a friend and then my lover—she was newly separated from her husband; she was the mother of four-year-old Rebecca and on her own for the first time in her life.

I remembered the intense and brief relationships I had formed after my own first marriage broke up a few years earlier, so I moved very gently into Bonnie's life. We shared sandwiches in the park at lunchtime for weeks before I even suggested that we meet for a drink after work. I spent two weeks away during the summer, daydreaming about her, speaking to her frequently on the phone; and then I returned for our first dinner date and the beginning of a love affair that lasted twenty-three years.

What everyone remembers about Bonnie is the warmth of her welcome. She treasured dozens of friends, kept track of their lives, their jobs, their children, their birthdays, their celebrations and their heartbreaks. When friends were absent, she thought about them, wondered about their lives, wrote notes to them; and when she saw them again, she picked up the friendships as if no time had passed at all. At Bonnie's first memorial service were two women she had met in grade school and kept as friends for fifty years.

Bonnie formed lasting relationships wherever she worked, and she chose work that gave her deep satisfaction. When we fell in love, she was a fundraiser for the National Trust for Historic Preservation. A few years after we married, she returned to school, earned a master's degree in speech-language pathology and then spent twelve years treating patients who had suffered strokes and head injuries. Her commitment to her patients and the rapport she formed with them inspired admiration and even amazement in her colleagues. A senior speech pathologist recalled, "The first time I observed Bonnie conducting a therapy session, I was blown away—she was such a skilled and intuitive clinician. I remember having the most difficult time coming up with any suggestions for another method that she might try or some way in which she might refine her skills." At that time, Bonnie was still a student.

Two and a half years before she died, Bonnie changed careers again. She decided she had time for one more career before we both retired, and she wanted to be involved in protecting the environment. She became a major gifts officer for the National Parks Conservation Association. Helping to preserve and protect the national parks excited her. During the two years of treatment for cancer, she was always determined to get back to work as soon as possible, often before I thought it was a good idea.

Bonnie's idealism pushed her to work hard and to dedicate herself to other people's happiness. Everyone around her benefited from that; but sometimes it kept her from indulging herself as fully as I knew she deserved. She loved entertaining people at our home, but she rarely did it on the spur of the moment, because she wanted the house to be in perfect shape before people came in. Because she measured herself by the highest standards she could find, she often found herself lacking. One person might travel more than she did, another undertook home renovations that Bonnie and I shied from. Another was more active in volunteer work than she was, or seemed to read more books or create art that Bonnie could not.

Her sense of not being active enough, bold enough, energetic enough, creative enough played a shadowy counterpoint to the life that delighted her and inspired admiration in others. The outpouring of love I heard as people spoke at her two memorial services would not have surprised Bonnie; she knew she was loved. But I think she would have been startled at how much she was admired.

She was a person, I think, who underestimated herself. This made her easy to be around but did not make it easy for her to be happy. One day, early in her treatment for cancer, I went into our room and found her in bed, a book in her lap and tears on her cheeks. The book she was reading suggested that people who love life are more likely to survive cancer than those who don't. She said, "I don't know if I'm a person who loves life."

Yet this person who did not know if she loved life went through two abdominal surgeries and two brain surgeries. She did a month of daily infusions and, when that failed, chose the most devastating chemotherapy available—three rounds of a five-drug protocol spread over four months of her life. And through all, she inspired love and admiration in everyone who cared for her, because her appreciation of them, her determination to live her life, and her will to be well were so strong.

And yet, she doubted that she was a person who loved life.

Throughout the two years she was living with cancer, Bonnie wanted to get back to work. She wanted to attend her book club meetings and the symphony and chamber concerts. She wanted to cook for Rebecca and me. She wanted the normal life we'd had before she got sick. The more dangerous the cancer became, the more she prized normal life.

She resisted doing anything special just because she was sick. When she was fully recovered from the first brain surgery, we went to Italy for ten days. We did that not because she felt time was getting short, but because we had not been able to go to Europe the year before, and her returning strength seemed to offer an opportunity. Because she didn't want to take more than a week away from work—after being out so many weeks for treatment—it was a whirlwind trip.

She and I rarely talked about what might happen. Speculation didn't seem useful; there was so much to deal with in the present that pulling fears from an unknown future seemed ridiculous. Early on, she wondered aloud if she was denying to herself that this cancer might kill her. I answered that we knew it was hanging over our head, but we didn't need to walk around looking up at it. She seemed to accept that, and for most of the next two years we kept our eyes focused on what was right ahead of us, not what loomed over us.

In the first nine months of 2002, Bonnie had breezed through two brain surgeries. She had been to Italy, she had taken a week to visit her family and our summer cottage in Michigan. She was back at work. In September, she had some bad days but insisted on going to work. On October 1st, she got a ride to work from Rebecca, who protested that Bonnie should be staying home. At noon a colleague called me: Bonnie had gotten dizzy and fallen.

When I went to get her, she had difficulty walking out of her office to the car. We hoped that it was just swelling from the Gamma Knife procedure that had vaporized a tiny third tumor in her brain a few weeks before. At 5:00 I took her to the emergency room with an excruciating headache. A CAT scan showed severe brain swelling. At 11:00, while waiting for transfer to the intensive care unit, she lost consciousness. Only the fast intervention of the ER team saved her life.

Two days later, an MRI showed a diffuse tumor spread across the back of her brain. The neurosurgeon told us he could do nothing. Our oncologist told me to think of her remaining life in weeks, not months.

Three projects occupied Bonnie during the last weeks of her life. One was to do all her Christmas shopping. She and Rebecca got on the phone and ordered gifts, and she sent Rebecca off to stores to pick things up. All the gifts were bought, wrapped and shipped by the time she died, a week before Christmas.

The second project was to plan her own memorial service. She met with the Unitarian minister who had performed the marriage of my cousin the previous spring. She left Rebecca and me a list of people from her life whom we should ask to speak, and she made it clear that there should be lots of time for other people to say whatever they wanted to say. She said she wanted our friends Steve Silverman and Nina Falk to play music, as they had delighted her many times with their concerts. This was the plan that Rebecca and I followed for our memorial service just before Christmas and that her former colleagues at the National Rehabilitation Hospital followed for their own memorial service six weeks after Bonnie died. Each time, a portrait of Bonnie emerged from the hearts of those who loved and admired her.

Bonnie's third and last project was to write letters to Rebecca and me that we would read after she died. She did this when her strength was waning, and she told me in the last week of her life that she didn't have the strength to copy her drafts over. I feel blessed that she could not make this letter as impeccable as she wished. For me, the paper I have, with insertions and strikeovers showing how she filled out her thoughts, and the ragged handwriting revealing how she struggled to leave me this last message about her love and our life together, is far more precious than any neatly copied letter could possibly be.

"It's time to say good-bye now. Thank you for making my life so wonderful. I love you so much and I will always be with you in spirit. With love forever."

What Happens When You Let Go of Hope?

INSIGHTS creep up on me. Time and again, after Bonnie died, I would come to a realization that in retrospect seemed obvious, even though I had lived through months or years without seeing it.

One such insight came to me on the back porch of our summer house in Michigan, six months after Bonnie died. I had been thinking about the turns my life had taken, and as I was going out the back door, I recognized for the first time what had happened to hope over the two years of Bonnie's illness.

When she was first diagnosed with a rare melanoma that had already spread to lymph nodes in her abdomen, her chances of surviving more than five years were narrow, but real. She specifically chose not to look at sur-

vival statistics. With Internet searching and a word proces-
sor, I could edit medical articles before passing them on
to her, so she didn't even see where I had removed the
statistics. But I knew: five-year survival somewhere between
twelve and twenty percent. Bad odds, but some people like
her would beat the cancer. I had a real hope that she would
be one of those.

Over the next two years, real hope dwindled—with the
failure of the first treatment, the appearance of new metas-
tases, the first brain tumor, the second brain tumor.

And in October, when she nearly died as her brain
swelled in reaction to a widespread, inoperable tumor, the
last tiny star of hope winked out.

At the time I was a little surprised that the news did
not overwhelm me. After all, hadn't all my hope been
smashed? I thought I'd had hope right up to the moment
when the surgeon told us he was helpless to do anything
more, and the oncologist told me that I should think of
Bonnie's remaining life in weeks, not months. What had
really been going on with my hope was more subtle, and
it wasn't till that moment in Michigan that I saw it clearly.
Gradually, the narrow but genuine hope had dwindled,
replaced by a determined optimism or what I have called
"manufactured hope." This is the hope you speak out loud,
or share tacitly with the person you are losing. To all appear-
ances, I had the same amount of hope, but more and more
of that was manufactured. Only a tiny spark of real hope
remained—the hope for a miracle—and that spark winked
out on October 3rd.

This insight about hope cast a new light on the task that lay before me—the grieving, the healing.

You see, as I wandered through those disoriented weeks after Bonnie died, I thought that healing my grief would mean returning to the kind of life I had before Bonnie died. In this vision, I had been thrown for a loop by her death, but I could get back on my feet and be "normal," as I had been before she died.

In Michigan, half a year later, I saw that even before her death, even before she was diagnosed as terminal, I had long been living without hope. In Michigan, I recognized that my path through grief was not taking me back to the way I was before Bonnie died; it was taking me back to the way I was before she got sick, before hope started fading from my life.

For nearly a year, I took comfort from this insight: I had to go back to the way I had been, hopeful and thinking about the future, before Bonnie got sick. And months later, writing about this comforting insight, I saw that it was an illusion.

It's an illusion to believe that we ever go back at all. It's not just that I can't get Bonnie back—it's that losing Bonnie and knowing that I would lose her have taught me something about being present to life, and this lesson has altered my life forever. There is no recovering, no going back. The only way to go is forward, irreversibly altered by love and loss.

As HOPE FADED, what remained for me was an intense presence to my life with Bonnie. We both had a consuming involvement with her treatment, certainly; but we also found an unprecedented presence to our love for each other.

I counted myself as a good husband, but I had never been so intensely focused on Bonnie's wishes, her comfort and discomfort, the quality of her life, our life. As deeply as I loved Bonnie, I have a long habit of solitude, built up over thirty years of working solo as a freelance writer. It's natural for me to stand apart from people, looking on at the conversations, just as it was natural for Bonnie to engage people, to open her heart to them and inspire them to open their hearts to her. The two years of Bonnie's illness challenged me to be engaged in her life as never before.

One day in September, we were at the hospital all day for a Gamma Knife procedure. During one of the long spells of waiting, while the surgeon and the technician programmed the exact path and strength of the radiation, I was helping Bonnie back from the bathroom and onto the examining table. Our nurse, Felicia, walked into the room and burst into tears. Startled, we asked her why she was crying. She answered, "You love each other so much."

What brought Felicia to tears, I believe, was our intense focus on our present love for each other, a focus that grew out of not knowing what the future might be. As our hope for a future together faded, we came face to face with a truth that forms the basis of Buddhist belief—that only the present is real, that we can live our lives only in the eternal present.

My intense presence to life continued after Bonnie died. There were times when I could not imagine my future, and Bonnie seemed to have taken my whole past with her. That left me in a present that was deeply sad but overwhelmingly real, with my love for Bonnie as present as it had ever been. This intense presence appears to be a lasting gift: Since she died, my life and my world have appeared more precious and in sharper focus than ever before.

Bonnie's ashes are scattered on two hillsides facing each other across a stream spanned by an old bridge. I went there many times during the months after she died. I have never before paid such attention to the unfolding of a place in spring. I noticed how the beech trees along the shore bring out their leaves wrapped up as little brown torpedoes, and how one nameless shrub comes out with its leaves deeply grooved, like miniature Victorian ruffles. And what other year have I noticed that the downy serviceberry is the first tree to bloom in these eastern woods?

In grieving for Bonnie, I opened my eyes and ears to the world around me, and I opened my heart to experience a world of feelings within me.

Holding you,
I held our future tight.
When my arms were empty
I looked for the past
But you had carried it off.
I have learned
I love you
Now.

Loving Your Grief

GRIEF is how loving her feels. My grief is, in fact, nothing more or less than my love for her.

This conviction was with me from the start. I didn't figure it out, I just knew it. So on the front of the program we made for Bonnie's memorial service, I wrote these words:

> *Our love for you spreads its wings so wide*
> *That in soaring it blocks the sun.*
> *And when this shadow passes over us,*
> *We call it grief.*

One reason I came instinctively to this view of grief as love is that I had been grieving over Bonnie for ten weeks before she died. At the time, I didn't call it grief, but now I see clearly that I was grieving for Bonnie as I cared for her after her cancer became incurable. What was I doing but grieving when Bonnie described the memorial service she wanted us to hold for her, or when I went with her to the church where she wanted her service held? Like so many things that seem obvious to me in retrospect, it didn't occur to me then that planning a funeral service is a ritual of grief, even if the subject of the funeral is still with you. It didn't occur to me that I was grieving over the loss of her life . . . and so was she. Knowing that she would soon die, I grieved for her while I could still hold her, care for her, tell her how I loved her.

I had drawn insights about the nature of emotions like grief from Thich Nhat Hanh's book, *Peace Is Every Step,* which offers a way to transform anger, fear and other difficult feelings. It is best, he says, not to try to drive the feeling away as if it is not part of us. He advises us, rather, to embrace the feeling, "like a mother tenderly holding her crying baby."

"Feeling his mother's tenderness, the baby will calm down and stop crying. . . . A mother holding her baby is one with her baby. . . . So don't avoid your feeling. Don't say, 'You're not important, you're only a feeling.' Come and be one with it."

During the two years we tried to save Bonnie from cancer, *Peace Is Every Step* helped me deal with my fear and my wakeful nights. By the time she died, I was accustomed to embracing painful emotions as part of myself. Grief was not some alien feeling that had taken over me, some parasitic species living inside me and sapping my life. Grief was me, loving Bonnie in sadness and loss.

Seeing my grief as my love left me whole. I was deeply, deeply sad, emotionally exhausted beyond anything I'd ever experienced; but I was not possessed by an alien feeling that I wanted to cut out of me or poison with drugs. I was, simply, a man in love who would never again hold in my arms the woman I had loved for so many years.

In fact, grief had begun long before that terminal diagnosis, though I did not recognize it. Sometime in those two years, while hope was imperceptibly slipping away, I began grieving for the cloudless life we had had, grieving over the pain, the fear and the constant preoccupation with medical care that now filled our life. And as treatment after treatment failed, as the cancer appeared in more dangerous places, I mourned the loss of our future together, which we would not have.

In the end, there was no sharp line between loving her in life and grieving for her in death. I loved her and grieved for her as I held her; I loved her and grieved for her when she was gone.

Because I knew my grief as my love, I expected my grief to feel different as time went on, just as my love for Bonnie had changed from year to year. And so it did. My love for her was sometimes so deeply sad that it sucked all the energy out of me. Other times it was easier to bear. In time, I came to find the sweetness of my memories of Bonnie.

Grief is how my love feels. When it was hard to bear, I wanted my love to feel different, but I would not lose my love in order to lose my grief. One day I invented a fable about that:

Once there was a man who had lost his wife, whom he loved so deeply that his grief seemed unbearable. As days became weeks and weeks became months, he prayed to be released from his grief. One evening, taking a tortured walk in the woods near his house, he met a stranger standing in his path. The stranger said, "I can answer your prayer. I can take away all of your grief."

The grieving husband was skeptical, but felt a surge of hope.

"Simply drink this," said the stranger, pulling a small bottle from his pocket. "You will have no memory of your wife; it will be as if she never existed. And your grief will vanish."

The husband recoiled in horror. "Forget her? Forget my love for her? What kind of demon are you?" He turned and ran back through the forest to his home.

As he stirred up the fire in his hearth and looked at the little picture of his wife that he kept on the mantel, he searched in his heart for that familiar grief. When he felt it, he noticed that the feeling was not nearly so sad; in fact his grief glowed softly with a warmth that was a great deal like love.

Passion, Loss, Beauty

CARING for Bonnie in the last months of her life transformed the way I lived my own life. I stopped working, so I could give all my time to being with her. My clients and friends helped in countless ways.

I lived each day focused on Bonnie, on being with her when she was feeling well, cherishing her life and helping her enjoy it. With Rebecca, I stayed by her when she was sick or undergoing palliative treatments.

All this happened without question. Clients understood, colleagues helped fulfill obligations I could not. The way I live my life was transformed with a few phone calls.

When I realize how many people helped make that possible, or adjusted to that sudden change, I am amazed and overwhelmed with gratitude. And I feel silly to have thought that big changes in life take time and planning and caution.

This change had none of those: It happened immediately, as soon as I said it aloud. And in the end I didn't come close to tapping all the resources that were offered or ready to be offered. It seems that people respond to tragedy. But tragedy is just the story that gives them their cue that they should respond.

What people really respond to is passion. And what I mean by passion is a total, immediate commitment to what is happening in the present.

FOR MOST of my life, it never occurred to me that one day I would have to tell my wife that she was dying. If I had looked ahead, especially during the last year of Bonnie's life, I could have anticipated that I would have to do that. After all, in January of 2002, I'd had to wait alone in my house for an hour, waiting for Bonnie to come home so I could tell her she had a brain tumor.

I might have anticipated that someday I would have to tell her that the latest recurrence of her cancer was going to kill her. But in those years we met her illness a day at a time, a week at a time. We looked at what we knew we had to handle, what we could handle right now, not what we might encounter that we weren't ready to meet.

In October of 2002, I knew for two days, while Bonnie recovered in intensive care, that when she woke up and was ready to hear it, I would have to tell her the news: Her life was about to end. I saw that coming, but I didn't know that I would have to tell her not once, but three times, and that Rebecca would have to break the news just as many times. Because of the trauma Bonnie's brain had suffered, she could ask what was happening to her before she could remember what we told her for more than a few minutes. So, over the course of three days, I gently broke the news to her each morning, and Rebecca did the same when she came in the afternoon.

Was it horrible to tell her that she was going to die? No, it was a conversation filled with tenderness and love.

One day, I watched Rebecca tell her mother that she would die. I saw a beauty that I never expect to see again, no matter how long I live. Becca's total focus on her mother, the intensity of her love as she watched Bonnie's reaction to her words—this is my lifelong image of life lived with passionate intensity.

Bonnie lies back, listening,
Embraced by Becca's gaze.
Each word of bad news is a loving stroke.
Speaking the news, the daughter is lit
with love that illuminates her mother.

Choosing the Unavoidable

➤ THERE was no question in Bonnie's mind that she was deeply loved.

Ultimately, though, being loved while being miserable was not enough. Bonnie chose to die.

Almost a year after her death, I was walking along a bike trail in Bethesda when I was struck by this thought: My love, deep as it was, was not enough to make Bonnie want to live. This was a humbling viewpoint, but also reassuring, in the way that leaning against a wall is reassuring. Whatever a wall may be keeping out or keeping in, it is solid, it is a limit. My love for Bonnie could not make her want to live past that Friday night. That night, our love encountered the wall that no love can go over, around or through.

The death that lay ahead for Bonnie was unavoidable. She would have died soon even if she had chosen to cling to her life of love and misery. Still, I believe that choosing death gave Bonnie peace, allowed her to give up her two-year struggle, allowed her to accept her humanity. Certainly, it has given me peace to know that she accepted what no one could change. I had worked for two years to keep her alive, and I'd failed. I had dedicated myself for ten weeks to help her get every possible good day out of her remaining life, and I think I succeeded, with Rebecca's help. But still, my love for Bonnie could not make her want to live past that Friday night.

She chose to die. If I love Bonnie completely as she was, then I must accept and love this choice of hers. If I love the Bonnie who chose death, then I must love her choice of death. In a sense, I must choose her death with her.

There's a wall around your love
that your love can't get over,
can't go around.
That good old mossy wall was there
before you came along,
the good old wall named death.

I wept before that wall,
pounded it,
roared at it.
And learned that love
can also sit on the grass and lean against that wall
without failure, without blame.
It's just a wall that's been there always,
and your love can sit alone on the grass,
lean against that wall
and rest.

Coming to a Stop

ONE day not long after Bonnie died, as I was walking home from the subway, my steps became slower and slower, till I came to a stop.

I didn't decide to do this. It was just that I completely lacked motivation to keep walking. There was no reason to stop on that stretch of sidewalk between Friendship Heights and my house and, it seemed, no reason to go on. I stood there for a few minutes, lost in a bemused reflection, with a lassitude through my whole body. This was not the fatigue that was very familiar those days. This was simply a loosening of the muscles, an absence of motivation to take the next step.

Eventually it was embarrassment, more than anything else, that made me begin moving, very consciously, left foot, right foot, till I was walking normally toward home.

I came to a stop again in Baltimore-Washington International Airport. I had dropped my aunt at an early plane. On the way out to the airport, I had seen the inbound morning-rush traffic backed up in the rain. Rather than sit in that traffic, I went looking for a place to have a cup of coffee, to think and write in my journal.

The airport was being reconfigured; I was walking down a corridor beside a temporary wall when once again I just came to a stop. I leaned against the wall, almost too slack to stand up. I was nowhere. I was in a dead-end corridor in an airport with no plane to catch, no one to meet, no one waiting at home.

A few people passed by. I don't know that anyone took notice, but again, it was embarrassment that got me started stepping out with one foot, then the other. I found a cafeteria where I sat with a cup of bad coffee, listening to smarmy country songs on the ceiling speakers. Smarmy songs that brought me to tears.

These episodes remained mere anomalies till nearly a year later, when I was walking on the Capital Crescent Trail, reflecting on what I might say in this book. I stopped, looking ahead at the inviting prospect of that wooded trail, thinking about whether it was time to turn around. At a dead stop, I had no momentum forward or backward. I was poised to move in either direction, in any direction, and I had a new insight into those moments of immobility months before.

Perhaps some instinct in me was protesting my dead,

rote, step-by-step persistence. Somewhere in me was a need to choose a new direction. That need brought me to a stop. It brought me to a position of stillness from which I could go in any direction. I didn't pick up the cue. At the time, the only direction I could think to go in was the direction I had been going. The only life I could imagine was the life I had been living when Bonnie was with me. I had to do it now without her.

In early spring, around the time these incidents occurred, my friend Rob Smith visited me and told me about another of his friends who had lost his wife; that friend took advantage of the forced change to make new choices about his career. He simply threw out all his assumptions, the old decisions that he had been carrying out, happy enough with them as long as his love for his wife made his life content. Without her to make the old routine seem worthwhile, he discarded it and started from scratch. Rob offered to help me examine my work, my life, whatever I wanted to change, and coach me to set new goals, take on new ventures.

Rob's instinct was right. My own instinct, which brought me to a point of zero momentum, was right. But the timing was all wrong. At the time those things happened and those opportunities were offered, my energy was so low that the familiar was all I could undertake. At least, that's what I felt.

In those first weeks and months after Bonnie died, plugging on seemed the only possibility. Plugging ahead was reassuring, as if everything had not changed when she died.

Plugging on seemed the easiest thing to do, yet it drained me. Not only that, it left me feeling that this was all I would ever be able to do. Desperation rose like a fog from that thought.

Months later, when I was actually engaged in making a new life, those incidents of coming to a stop, those moments of stillness, struck me as early invitations from deep within myself to start new.

Stillness contains infinite possibility. When my body said "stop," it did not mean "go nowhere." At a stop, any direction is possible. Stillness encompasses all directions, motionlessness encompasses all motions.

As I see it today, this coming to a stop was an instinctive inner sit-down strike against going on with my eviscerated life. It was a protest that the life I had lived with Bonnie had ended at her death; that without her, plodding on was senseless. I needed to invent something new.

I was not ready to do it. I didn't know I could do it. So I put one foot in front of the other and kept going. Only much later did I realize how easy it was to accept the invitation to choose a new life.

A man comes to a stop
beside a semi-permanent wall.
Suitcase-wheels whir past.
He has no plane to catch,
and no one waits at home.

Death has brought him to a standstill.
Grief has brought him to a stop.
Emptied of momentum,
His stillness is death's mirror image.

But stillness unbiased to any direction
embodies all directions.
All futures.
All lives.
All life.

Ritual

WHEN I first started thinking about ritual, I had stereotypes to overcome. "Ritual" spoke to me of incense and High Mass, baptism and confirmation, rituals I once revered and had left behind. Looking back with a more open mind, I see that my life after Bonnie was full of rituals, and I wonder if I could have eased my sorrow by trusting more to their power.

Originally, I didn't even think of Bonnie's memorial services as a ritual. At a Unitarian church, free-form, designed by Bonnie's wish, it seemed the opposite of the fixed forms of Catholic ritual I had grown up with. It was merely a chance for people to remember Bonnie, to speak of her, to take some time for reflection on who she had been and what she meant to us. Some time to give her the honor we felt she was due.

I didn't call it a ritual then. Now I think that's exactly what ritual is.

I think a ritual is any practice that makes space for things that would otherwise be ephemeral and elusive. Rituals make space for important experiences that would otherwise be pushed aside by what we've decided is necessary or urgent.

Some of our funeral ritual is designed to keep us busy, to keep us moving, even by rote, to fill days that would otherwise be endlessly empty. These, it seems to me, are the rituals of numbness, and numbness can be a merciful friend.

Early on, numbness protects us. Activity keeps our focus away from the depth of our loss, as motion keeps a water-skier from sinking. At Christmas, Becca and I went through the motions, she with her family and I with mine. A day or two later, still protected by numbness, we opened the presents Bonnie had bought for us.

At New Year's, I attended a dinner hosted by my friend Sheila, whose husband Tom had died with thunderous suddenness one day before Bonnie. Holding that New Year's dinner was Sheila's act of determination, and it served both her and me well. When all the other guests had left, three of us who had lost spouses in 2002 talked by ourselves, struggling to make peace with our losses and hoping for a quiet night's sleep and a better day tomorrow.

Most of the time, early on, I skated over the depth of my loss by keeping busy. It was a way to shorten the bland, aching days, to get on to what I hoped would be better days beyond. Instinctively, though, I took some time to be with Bonnie. I lit a candle, mostly because Bonnie loved the way candles make an occasion special. I sat with pictures of her because I dreaded the fading of my memory. I cried if I could.

Ritual celebrates your choice to be with the person you have lost. You dedicate a place, you dedicate a time, maybe just a few minutes, but you dedicate those to being entirely with the person you love. That ritual is effective, whether the person is with you or absent. The ritual works if the person is living or dead. It works because you are intensely present to the person you love and you are intensely present to your love.

I WROTE that last paragraph almost exactly a full year after Rebecca and I walked over a little bit of land and dipped our hands into a container of ashes, all that was left of Bonnie's body. That was when we scattered her ashes over the two hillsides that face each other across a creek spanned by an old foot bridge. It was March, and there was nothing growing. The woods were brown and bare, and we had no idea how beautiful this spot would become—with white flowers on the downy serviceberry and the little dogwoods that you hardly notice when they're not in bloom, and the pale, pale pink of the native azaleas that line the road just by this bridge. (It's the same kind of native azalea that refused to bloom in our backyard the spring after Bonnie died, and one year later bloomed beautifully.)

When we scattered the ashes, the land was bare and brown and dry and cold. And we ourselves felt bare and cold. We were feeling the death in us, Rebecca and I, and hoping for spring to come, hoping for spring in us, hoping for something to be reborn. And it was. It was reborn.

Over the following months, I came often to Bonnie's bridge, several times a week when I was at my saddest. Being at the bridge still allows me to sink into Bonnie. It's a place where, in the best of circumstances, everything else goes away; I found myself coming to the bridge for that release. I could stand on the bridge and get the sense of being completely with her, a feeling I treasured then and still do.

In the best visits, I could come here and just be completely present to what I was holding of Bonnie, how I was holding her, how I was missing her. There was an energy, an alertness in my presence, an openness to everything that was here. Every bird coming along the creek was part of that experience of being here with Bonnie. I had an urge to know this place intimately, season by season. I could stare at the water pouring down through the chute between two boulders and be completely bound to this place. I was being also, somehow, completely with Bonnie, because this was the place we had dedicated as her place.

So the place embodies the ritual, doesn't it? It's the physical place where I can pay attention to her, and either because Bonnie had the power to arrange it that way, or because I was paying such intense attention to this place, wonderful things happened here.

One day there were tiger swallowtail butterflies that swooped around me and then followed me a half mile along the creek back toward the car. There was the great blue heron that flew over my head one day and on another day stood in the water watching for fish. There was the hawk that flew low over my head one summer afternoon. There is a healing power in the kind of attention I was paying, in being intensely present to Bonnie's place. There was a healing power in laying everything else down and being with all my feelings, all of my anguish. And being with my fear, if I couldn't lay that down. But fear is really about the future. So if you are really here, right now, really present, you can lay the fear down also.

One Sunday in early September, walking down the road to the bridge, I was practicing seeing things with complete presence, and I was practicing breathing with my hand on my heart, a friend's suggestion for calming myself when my heart is full. As I walked up the road, every tree stood out with its own personality, and I would stop before a tree, riveted, as if I were staring at a gorgeous woman or an ancient magical face. Whole hillsides on either side of the valley seemed vibrantly alive, and I was so present to them that it astounded me. On this magical day I wept for Bonnie, and the people who passed by were practically invisible to me. In this place that Rebecca and I chose to be Bonnie's, life was vibrating around me.

So is creating a dedicated time and space truly all you need from a ritual? Maybe it is. Maybe the gift of rituals is the gift of simple presence: A ritual makes you completely and honestly here, right now. That can bring deep relief from all the stirring around and talking and wrestling that we do with our emotions. If you give yourself the right ritual—something simple like standing on a bridge with water running under you, or sitting in front of a candle with a picture of that beloved person you are never going to see again—it is so simple. There is absolutely nothing for you to do but to be there. And that is a tremendous gift.

Now that I have come to this broad embracing definition of ritual, I see that it reaches back to include caring for Bonnie after we knew she would die. During those ten weeks, there was nothing we could do to change the outcome; nothing could prevent her death, and we probably couldn't even push back the day. But something was within our power: We could pull away, or we could be fully, completely present. Just in caring for her, in holding her hand and helping her down the stairs or up the stairs, or helping her out of the bed to the bathroom—every one of those actions made Becca and me as present to Bonnie as we could be. I was present to her in a way that I had rarely achieved, much as I loved her. All those rituals of care made me know how much I loved her. I hope that, wrapped in her illness and her weakness, she was present to it also.

When I stopped working so that I could take care of Bonnie, I thought the time would be about other things, too, like doing things around the house that Bonnie wanted to see finished. For example, I thought I would construct a built-in bookcase in the family room, which I had planned and never gotten around to. During those two months that

I was home with Bonnie, it didn't get done, because that time was not about building things. That time and that place were not even about taking care of her, though I did that and Rebecca did that.

That time and that place were all about loving her and being completely with her. Completely with her. Everything else was just the accompanying circumstances. So you could see that as a two-month ritual, a time and a place set aside so that the ephemeral thing called Bonnie's life could be all we thought about, all that mattered, and nothing else could intrude.

I would have said at the time that I was taking those two months off for Bonnie. The fact is, it was an immeasurable gift to myself to lay down all other concerns, all practical considerations, and allow myself to concentrate on the one person in the world who was more important to me than any other. The ritual consisted of setting aside that time and all of our home to Bonnie, to caring for Bonnie, and to loving Bonnie as long as she would be with us. That ritual was the greatest gift I had ever given myself.

The ritual of coming to Bonnie's bridge has given me a way to come back to what I learned and what I felt, a way to come back to how I loved Bonnie, how I still love her. It's given me a place where all this is still real, a place I can touch with my physical senses, a place I can see and hear and smell and feel under my feet, while those other intangible senses of memory and heart and knowing and thought all reach out to her and bring her into my consciousness.

Give yourself the gift of ritual.
Clear away a little of the eternal now,
set aside one place in the vast universe
where nothing happens
except your love for the one you lost.

Undertow

FATIGUE may be the most common manifestation of grief. I reacted to fatigue by plodding on, staying occupied if not busy—by going gradually back to work.

Then one day, my colleague Ann Herzog spoke a few words that conveyed the most useful information on grief I ever heard from anyone.

"Grief is like undertow," she said. "Whatever you try to do, it pulls against you."

I couldn't imagine a better description of the weight I felt dragging at me as I tried to keep plodding ahead through my daily life. And Ann added a prescription that went with this:

"If you fight the undertow all the time, you'll exhaust yourself. Sometimes you just have to rest, stop fighting and let the undertow carry you for a while."

Letting the undertow carry me took many forms over the next several months. Often it took the form of lighting a few candles on the coffee table in the living room and sitting with a picture of Bonnie, with my memories. It took the form of writing in my journal . . . or sitting with my journal open and not writing a word. Later it took the form of standing on the bridge where Bonnie's ashes are scattered and being alone with my thoughts of her.

Ann said another thing that was invaluable to me as I lived with my grief. "You're using an emotional energy you don't even know about."

Time and again, I have seen that I am doing emotional work somewhere deep inside me. Though I can choose to ignore it, I can't stop it. It is me loving Bonnie and coming to terms with losing her.

Sometimes I was able to ignore what was going on— when I felt better, when work or friends engaged my attention. But when I ignored the intense emotional work that I was doing, when I let it happen automatically and unacknowledged, I soon found that my ability to concentrate began to diminish. I would struggle to do some simple piece of mental work. I would sit at my desk, shuffling endlessly through papers that needed filing away, clicking idly from one Internet site to another.

To restore my ability to concentrate on my day-to-day life, I had to pay attention to my love for Bonnie, to spend time with the memories and the feelings that are what I have of her.

I had a precious resource for healing: a family summer place that I had visited some twenty-two years with Bonnie, including the summer before she died. This place was full of memories of Bonnie—things we had done together there, the little red kayak that was her favorite boat. The décor of the cottage, which had barely changed through most of my life, now bore her mark. More remarkably, the new décor was a monument to her ability to inspire agreement among three generations of the families that shared the cottage.

What made the summer cottage uniquely powerful for healing was that it's a place where I came most summers of my life before I knew Bonnie and expect to come for many summers more.

As soon as I walked in the kitchen door of that cottage, I was enveloped by memories of Bonnie, and also by memories of thirty-five summers before I knew and loved her. I remember being here with her. I remember being here without her the summer I was first falling in love with her. I remember being here years upon years before I even knew she existed. Here, in the memories and associations of one place, was a panorama of my life that encompassed Bonnie, yet stretched back through all the decades when she had not yet come into my life. Here I expected to spend many summers in the expanse of my life that I was to live without her once again.

Bonnie was not the only one who was missing from that cottage. The year before, six months before Bonnie's death, my mother had died, suddenly but not unexpectedly, at eighty-six. The last summer Bonnie came to the cottage was also my father's last visit (he had first come there in 1919). Bonnie and I had watched him sitting alone; we had taken him to the emergency room when his medical problems flared up. We were not surprised when he said he would not come again.

So I slept in the bed where Bonnie and I had slept, I puttered in the shop that my father had tried to keep organized. I stepped, briefly, into the little cottage out back that my parents had used for thirty summers, built by my father's mother as a sanctuary in the later years of her own life.

To spend a month with all these reminders of lost and absent family was amazingly comforting. Here I was, remembering Bonnie and my mother and my grandmother and grieving for all the loss in my life. And yet it seemed natural in this cottage, which had outlasted many of its owners, that people would come and depart. It seemed natural that lives would end and lives would go on.

The perspective I gained simply by walking in the door of that old summer cottage had a tremendous healing effect on me. Without diminishing in the least my love for Bonnie, it placed her life and mine into a larger continuum of time. Members of my family came here before I was born and will, I expect, come here long after I am gone. We are, after all, beings who shine for a while and then disappear. This place allowed me to see that Bonnie's coming and her going, as beautiful and heartbreaking as they were, were in the natural order of life.

I was describing this impact to my brother Frank, a psychologist. He commented that in treating emotional trauma, psychologists try to take the patient back to a time before it happened, take them through the trauma and then into the future after the trauma is over. He said it seemed that I had had that healing treatment just by walking in the door!

My month-long respite—from the house where Bonnie and I made our home and from the routine of work that had sustained our life together—allowed me to coast with the undertow when I needed to, to exercise and do some work, and to spend all the time with my memories of Bonnie that I needed to. It was a time of deep healing; I returned home eager to create a new way of living. My love for Bonnie was still more sad than joyful. But grief was no longer the central theme of my life, and the undertow had released its grip.

What does "never" mean? You've always known,
but after months alone, you live it.

You're long past the ascetic sting,
the blasting of eternal sands
as you held your dying darling's hand.

Now flat, astringent days break like waves.
Muscling past you, swimming or adrift,
they haul you and exhaust you.

Scratched in hard dirt is your defense, your plan
to live alone under lingering clouds that rarely rain.
Bare necessities you scavenge from the wreck,
and nights you sleep wrapped tight
to leave no tender part exposed.

Helping

❧ OVER the years since Bonnie died, I've had some heartfelt conversations with people who wonder how to be most helpful to a friend who has lost a parent or a spouse, or to someone who is caring for a terminally ill patient.

At a birthday dinner party, I was seated next to a young woman named Renée, who wondered how to be helpful to a friend whose husband is dying of a brain tumor. Her question took me back to those two years when we were living with Bonnie's illness. It reminded me of the many ways people helped, the ways they tried to help, and the many different reactions we had to their attempts.

My first answer to Renée's question about how she could be helpful was, "Ask."

Looking back over those two years, I know that no one could have guessed what we wanted from our friends, because what we wanted changed from week to week.

People said to us, over and over, "If there's anything we can do, please just ask." We rarely asked for anything because there was little we needed, except an impossible cure. But though we did not take them up on their offers, knowing that we could ask created a space of safety for us that was a continual gift, day in and day out.

There was only one friend, for example, who was welcome in Bonnie's hospital room, both because she was such a close friend and because she worked at another hospital across the street. When Chris came to visit, Bonnie felt perfectly comfortable sending her away or falling asleep while Chris sat there. Because Chris was a speech pathologist like Bonnie, Bonnie didn't worry that Chris would be shocked by her condition—they both had treated patients far worse off than Bonnie was.

When Bonnie almost died of swelling in her brain and was in intensive care as they diagnosed the tumor that would prove fatal, my first two calls were not to my brother or my father. I knew that each of them would be heartbroken to hear Bonnie was in trouble. Instead, I asked my cousin Bob to come to the hospital. He arrived at the intensive care unit with a book that looked to be 1,500 pages long and said, "I'll be in the waiting room if you need anything."

I called my colleague and friend Susan to let her know about Bonnie and gratefully accepted her offer to come to the hospital. Between them, these two could handle notifying almost anyone in our diverse worlds of friends, family and business associates. These two people, from different parts of my life, just seemed to be the right people to have with me then. In fact, any of a hundred people would have come as quickly and lovingly. I needed people around me then whom I did not need to look after.

In fact, through those whole two years, we leaned on only a handful of people out of the hundred or more who offered. So here was Renée, asking for my advice on how to be helpful. Here is what I told her:

Make sure your friend knows she can call you for anything. Even if she never calls, knowing that she can will be a comfort.

Let her know, if she says she's okay, that you really hear that she is okay. (I have a friend who would not accept that, who insisted on finding out how I was not okay. I ended those conversations feeling invaded.) People can be okay in the midst of dying. People can need nothing when they are losing everything they value most. Do not let your wish to sympathize stop you from hearing the truth, and don't let your wish to help appear as her obligation to let you help.

I also told Renée that a few people, who were not in a position to help, made unforgettable gifts by sending cards or notes every few weeks. Two nieces, an old friend and a new colleague used this simple gesture to be present in the gentlest possible way. This was especially good for Bonnie, who loved to send and receive notes and cards.

At some points, when Bonnie was very sick, neighbors brought food. We appreciated the gesture and soon had to cut off the supply as the refrigerator was full, Bonnie was eating no more than a little soup, and Rebecca does not eat meat. So the support was important and so was our ability to say, "That's enough."

During Bonnie's last weeks, the three of us were self-sufficient. For most of the time, Bonnie needed little care. At first she slept most of the day, with Rebecca's cat, Reuben, curled up on her chest or behind the crook of her knee. When she was awake for more of the day, her parents, sister and brother came for what we all knew would be their last visit with her. Then Bonnie got stronger; she wanted to cook as usual. She napped, she planned her memorial service, she did her Christmas shopping with Becca.

Then her strength began to fade. We three hunkered down; we did what needed to be done, what could be done. Even when there was nothing that anyone could do for us, knowing how many people would do *anything* for us—that let us feel safe, so we could be completely present to Bonnie in those last precious days. On the Sunday before she died, Bonnie was incommunicative and restless; her breathing was irregular, and we worried that she might be in pain. In the morning, Rebecca called her uncle's wife Karen, a nurse, who dropped everything, drove an hour from Annapolis, helped and reassured us, knew when to leave us alone with Bonnie, and refused to leave until Bonnie's sister arrived from Michigan late that evening.

Sometimes support was crucial; sometimes privacy was more important. When Bonnie first started treatment for cancer, she welcomed the support and sympathy that poured out to her. Every month or two, I would send an e-mail to a circle of friends, just to let them know that

Bonnie was home from the hospital, or about to have surgery, or back to work. This saved a lot of calling around and repetitious reports. After Bonnie's first brain surgery, though, she began to prize her privacy and to work harder at living her normal life. She asked me to stop sending e-mails. Anyone who did not need to know details was to be told that she had more surgery, period. I believe she had noticed the alarm in someone's eyes when she said "brain tumor." She told me she didn't want her life to be about cancer.

So she shifted from prizing the offers of help to wishing people would treat her just as if she were well. But we didn't have much energy to be concerned about others. If they felt helpless, we needed them to deal with that themselves.

For most of the people who would have loved to help us, the true answer was, "There's nothing we need you to do." But the sincere offers gave us a pervasive sense of safety, of being held and cared for, of people waiting to give help if we should need it.

> *I am losing everything that matters*
> *And I am OK.*
> *Everything is being taken from us,*
> *And we need nothing.*
> *I will never call on you*
> *And knowing that I can*
> *Makes me feel safe.*

Gifts

BONNIE had been gone eleven months when my father decided to die.

He had been in a nursing home for six weeks on intravenous feeding after most of his small intestine was removed. Now his organs were failing, he had pneumonia, and he was ready to stop.

One gift that Bonnie's death gave me was that I was ready to help my father as he died. When I told my brother that I would take Dad out of the hospital and bring him to my house with hospice care, Frank thought about Bonnie dying in that same house and said, "I hope you know what you're doing."

The gift I had from Bonnie was that I knew exactly what I was doing: I was ready to help my father die in peace surrounded by love. That ability was a gift that Bonnie's illness and death had given me.

I made a call to hospice, and a young man visited Dad's hospital room to educate us about hospice care. When I told him what Bonnie and I had been through, he realized I already knew what he had come to tell us; so in the darkened room, while Dad slept, we talked about the young widow he was deeply in love with, and his confusion about how he could be in her life while she was still grieving for the husband she had lost. As he left, he thanked me for what I had been able to tell him about grief.

Bringing Dad home was more complicated than just setting up a hospital bed. It took four tanks of liquid oxygen connected with a maze of tubing to supply the amount of oxygen he needed. He arrived with a prescription for morphine that was practically impossible to fill late on a Saturday afternoon. The hospice staff handled all these challenges with unstoppable professionalism. The doctors had told us that Dad would last no more than a week. Six hours after he arrived at my house, he died.

So, among all the gifts Bonnie gave me, one was my ability to show my love for my father in the last few days of his life. For decades, it had been easier for my father and me to discuss objects and activities than to speak about deep emotions. For a long time, it had been Bonnie who spoke easily and lovingly to my parents, and I had allowed her to be my bridge to them.

In the eleven months when we were both widowers, my father and I didn't find much to say about our shared losses. He knew how much I had loved my mother. I remembered how wonderful Bonnie had been with him when Mom died, and I had seen in his eyes that losing Bonnie in the same year crushed his heart in a way he had no words for. Still, there was a reticence, a mute agreement that separated us.

Having depended on Bonnie to be the bridge, I felt inept at speaking to my father of the love I had for him. But in his last days, when he accepted death as she had, I found that Bonnie's life and her death had taught me what I needed to ease my father's death and to make sure that his life ended as hers had, surrounded by love.

Death is a teacher
I would never choose.
Yet we can choose
to use death's lessons
for the dying
and living.

The Omnipresence of Grief

✿ AS LONG as we live and grow, we will leave behind things, people and places we love. Every day we wake up, we have put another day into the past. Even if we move from joy to joy, we will find a place in ourselves that grieves for the joy that is gone. We grieve even for things that never happened—I have grieved deeply for the future that Bonnie and I will never have.

Denial of a grief doesn't really help. Whether someone tells me, "You should enjoy the good things you have," or I tell myself, "I have nothing to be sad about," denial simply pushes grief underground, where it can work anonymous mischief.

My mother, my wife, my father all died within a period of eighteen months. None of these deaths came out of the blue. I see now that while I was anticipating each of these deaths, I braced myself for the emotions I might feel. While that helped me to function, it also separated me from the grief I was feeling. I was able to tuck away a lot of my grief. In the end, I had to go looking for it.

I protected myself from grief by bracing myself for it, and right after Bonnie died, I protected myself with a numbness that mercifully prevented me from feeling how complete and permanent that loss was. A few months later I encountered another wave of sadness, when I allowed myself to know what "never" really means. Everyone who is grieving experiences good days and bad days, and I believe the bad days come when we instinctively allow ourselves to feel more, when we open another door, find another reminder, when we remember some other delight from our former life that we will never have again.

Something within me protects me from having to feel more than I could stand. And something in us knows that we're stronger than we believe. Though numbness shut me down at first, gradually I allowed myself to feel more of the sorrowful or painful love that I wanted to feel. Something in us wants to feel love, no matter how painful, no matter how sad; and if we keep our numbness in place, we pay a price that is far, far worse than feeling the sadness of our love.

I've learned that I, like most human beings, have a tremendous ability to partition myself. It's as if we tuck painful memories and emotions away somewhere in our being; then we declare that part of ourselves off-limits.

Paradoxically, I felt that Bonnie's death had ripped me open, put me in touch with my feelings in a way I never had been before. Certainly I had never felt any emotions as intensely as I felt that grief and love, and I had never given myself permission to speak so openly about my feelings as I did to my family and friends in the months after Bonnie died.

Still, freedom to speak about our emotions is not the same as the ability to feel them. Thousands of words poured out of me, touching other people with their passion. But I was good at speaking grief, not good at feeling it, releasing it. There was a tremendous emotion tucked away where it could not touch me, and I could not touch it.

Somewhere below the tears that choked in my throat, below the pang of sadness in my chest, there was howl of grief and fear that I could not release; I did not know how. In fact, I was afraid to release it. That howl of grief springs from the knowledge that death is forever, that grief is a fixture in human life. Perhaps it is so difficult to release because this howl comes from recognizing our utter helplessness. Though I longed to weep, only rarely did my grief emerge fully unleashed, as a howl.

Or perhaps I found that howl of grief so hard to release because I was raised by two models of self-control, two parents who believed that the measure of a man is not what he feels but what he does, and that unleashed emotion can cause devastation.

About a year after Bonnie died, I was able to release that howl for the first time, in a retreat led by Joy Davey and Lawrence Stibbards from the Shalom Mountain Retreat Center. I was amazed by the power of the howl I still held inside me at a time when I was happy, even joyful, in the new life I was creating. In later retreats, too, that howl was waiting to emerge. I have come to recognize that it's not only losing Bonnie that drives this cry; it's the loss of everyone and everything that has passed irretrievably from my life.

It's amazing how often I must remind myself to touch my grief, to give it some attention and some time to be felt. If I skate across the surface of my feelings, moving ahead with a life that is full of comforts and delights, that leads to living my life automatically, with only part of myself engaged, noticed and expressed. By loving and losing Bonnie, I have learned that there is much more to my life, much more to me, than strategies for keeping myself comfortable and safe.

I bring my love for Bonnie forward into my new life. I bring my grief, too. I can choose to accept or resist my grief, but I cannot end it, and I would not want to, because grief is the other face of love. It is the inevitable consequence of change . . . of life.

Now she will always be water,
and I will always be earth,
and there will always be a shoreline
where water touches earth,
caresses and softens it
until I melt
as she did.

Returning

A YEAR after we scattered Bonnie's ashes, there was again nothing growing on the hillsides by the bridge. Here and there you could see little brown buds starting to form on some of the bushes, and the hillsides were clear, because not much undergrowth survives the winter. They were just leaf-covered hillsides, the way they were when we scattered her ashes, littered with some fallen trees that are going back into the earth the way they're supposed to, going back to the earth the way Bonnie wanted to, because she saw that it was right. She saw that going back to the earth was the natural way of things. She saw that things begin and end, but also that they move in cycles.

Somewhere in this soil, somewhere under my feet, Bonnie's ashes were nursing growth. The contents of that little container of ashes, which didn't weigh much, are back in this place, and are part of life still, part of the living earth, part of growing, part of dying, part of the cycle that will continue as long as there is life.

Bonnie didn't want to be held, frozen, in any one place. She didn't want to be buried in a single grave which would mark a little tiny plot of land as her place, in some manicured cemetery that was only about death. She wanted her ashes to be scattered, she wanted to be dispersed back into life, into a living place that's about growing and blooming and falling down. She wanted to fall as naturally as a leaf does, and go back into the cycle of life as naturally as a leaf does.

Bonnie never wanted her life to be about cancer, and she didn't want her death to be about death. She wanted her death to be about being part of life. Her death was the end of her life, but it's become a part of my life, a part of Rebecca's life. Her death and the way she did it, the way she lived to the end of her life, that's become part of all of us; that's become part of what all her loved ones know about life.

I'm not sure we know very much about life, because we don't pay attention; but in the ritual of caring for Bonnie, in the ritual of grieving for Bonnie, in the ritual of being present and mindful of everything that she meant to us, we've learned a lot about life, and she keeps teaching it to us.

There's a bright colored baby's mitten on the bridge.
Somebody will have cold fingers by now.
They'd find it if they returned this way,
Since I've wedged it up in the railing post.
Probably they won't be back,
not looking for a little thing like that,
That can be replaced.
I return to this bridge for what
You can't replace.
I return looking for the wife I lost,
Knowing I can't replace her and can't find her,
Not here, not anywhere.
But I return to this bridge
And I find a baby's colorful mitten
And I find something of a love lost.
I do find something here.
So I keep making time
To return to this place
Time after time.

My Path

AFTER Bonnie died, looking at the new life of grief that had opened up ahead of me, I wanted to look at grief as a path from something to something. Surely this intense experience was taking me somewhere. But from where to where?

I desperately hoped it was a path that led away from overwhelming sadness to something more bearable. Clearly, it was a path that led away from the time before Bonnie died when I was consumed, overwhelmed, totally dedicated to loving her sadly and caring for her. It was a path that led away from the time after she died, when the sadness of loving her drained all my energy into the effort of fighting that undertow.

Before I lost Bonnie, I thought I knew what the path of my life was. When human beings believe we know what our path is, we are capable of making that path appear, most of the time. On the path we imagine, there are no surprises. But death vetoed my path; death reminded me that what I planned, what I imagined for my future with Bonnie, was simply an imagining, an illusion.

Our path began to narrow when Bonnie was first diagnosed with melanoma. We had to do what was necessary, we had to find doctors, learn about treatments. She had to go through the surgeries and the chemotherapy and the recovery. With each passing month and each recurrence of the cancer, life seemed to be steering us with an unrelenting command. It steered us through a year of surgery, infusions, injections, and three waves of wracking chemotherapy, then more surgery, more scans, more medication. The fact of cancer moved us forward, made our decisions for us, marked out our time, filled our calendar.

The final diagnosis of an inoperable brain tumor narrowed our path until all she and I could do was to take the good days that were given. All I could do was to cherish Bonnie and give her what she needed for each day, and finally be beside her as she died.

After she died, I imagined that my path was still narrow. It was as if I was walking along, looking down, focused only on the spot where I would place my foot next, not looking to one side or the other. I have taken one step, I can take another, I can put one foot out, then the next, and so on. Even when my friend Rob offered to help me create a new life, make new choices about my career that were long overdue, I felt I had no energy to take that on. More than that, I did not have the vision to see any direction I could go except straight forward, in the path I had been traveling.

I'm reminded of a day when Bonnie and I were driving around Provençe in 1997. We were driving out of the hills from Bonnieux, down a winding road hemmed in tightly by steep, rocky hillsides. Then, with the spectacular suddenness so typical of Provençe, we were out of the hills, out on a flat, straight road across the plain. Looking back, the time after Bonnie's death was like that emergence from the winding valley road—except that in this case I was so focused on my grief that I could not even appreciate how my path had suddenly widened.

So I continued to walk in that narrow path for a few months, wondering what I would do with my life. I didn't accept that I don't know where my path will lead. On the contrary, early on I struggled to imagine my future, what it would be like.

There was an edge of desperation in my daydreams. It seemed urgently important to know whether I would simply live alone, holding Bonnie's memory close and soaking up the sympathy of our friends and relatives. It seemed desperately important to know whether I, who had spent almost all of my adult life married or committed to women whom I would later marry, would in fact marry again. As I tried to imagine being with someone else, it seemed impossible that I could marry someone who hadn't known and loved Bonnie.

But death, by vetoing my plan and showing me what was truly impossible, also taught me a lesson about what is possible. It showed me that I had a choice, that I had always had a choice: I could give up imagining that the old path is the only path, and accept the overwhelming evidence that I do not know where my path is leading. Death showed me that I can accept not knowing and simply step forward with trust in myself, with trust in those around me, and trust in Providence.

If I had not come face-to-face with the truth that the life I had imagined with Bonnie is impossible, then I would not be standing here at this moment, knowing that futures in infinite variety are possible—for me to choose and for life to choose for me.

Before Bonnie got sick, my life was hemmed in with impossibilities I had created in my own mind. (It's impossible to change my career; it's impossible to afford a bigger house; it's impossible to move to another city.) Then I met true impossibility: to have Bonnie with me, to live out our lives as we planned—that was impossible.

When my life ran into that mammoth, real, rock-solid wall of impossibility called death, all of those imagined impossibilities showed up as pale, misty things of my imagination. All the "nevers" and impossibilities of my imagination were revealed as frauds, by the true "never," by the true impossibility that I encountered when I knew that Bonnie would die, and when she died.

THEN, to my complete astonishment, Carol appeared. When we were introduced as strangers, she somehow remembered that we had met casually, thirty-eight years earlier. Thinking I should follow up on this remarkable meeting, I invited her by e-mail to meet me for coffee. (I couldn't bring myself to phone her, because it felt like asking for a date.) When she didn't reply, because the e-mail disappeared into some Internet limbo, I was as much relieved as disappointed.

It wasn't till six weeks later that we spent a few hours together. I talked mostly about Bonnie, about loss and grief and the beautiful years we had together. Carol talked about the joys of her children, the sadness of marriages ending. She remembers listening to me that evening and hoping that someday someone would love her the way I loved Bonnie.

I remember waking up the next morning eager and optimistic about having made a new friend, with whom I could talk so freely about my love and grief for Bonnie. When I realized how long it had been since I had been both eager and optimistic about anything, I wept for half an hour. Three days later, leaving for my planned month in Michigan, I stopped at Carol's house to give her a goodbye hug. An hour later, I drove away, confused and reeling from the intensity of my feelings for her.

Not only had I not imagined falling in love with Carol, I had imagined it was impossible for me to fall in love with anyone while feeling such intense and immediate love for Bonnie. Over the course of a month away, I learned that a person has just one heart, and that one heart can be big enough to love two women wholeheartedly. Over the course of that month, I began to see my years with Bonnie in the context of my whole life and to find delight again in the sweetness of my memories of her. Almost every day, I paddled the little red kayak Bonnie loved, remembering how she reveled in the independence and solitude it gave her when she would disappear out on the lake for an hour or more. And almost every day I spent hours talking on the phone with Carol or reading and writing e-mails, as our love for each other deepened.

I'm a fortunate man: My path has brought me to a time of beauty and happiness. I am fortunate that I did not instinctively resist what seemed so improbable, even impossible and possibly lunatic—the idea that I would fall in love half a year after I lost the love of my life. I am fortunate that something in the way I loved Bonnie—had loved her and still love her—inspired me to trust the stranger I was falling in love with and to trust the love I was feeling for her. I trusted the new path that opened up to me. I also trusted my own instincts, even though I was falling in love with a speed and suddenness that alarmed some of my friends and relatives.

I don't know where this reservoir of trust came from. I've never thought of myself as a bold or courageous man, or as a man of faith; in my life I have not acted as a bold or courageous man. I have, for most of my life, played it safe, protected the people in my life and accumulated resources to keep my life secure. When, despite all that caution, I lost the one person who was most precious to me, I found myself face to face with the truth that safety is an illusion, or at least that safety, in the greatest sense, is completely out of our hands.

My path led me to a narrow, dark, and sorrowful place. There was nothing I could do to avoid passing through that place. Perhaps, facing that moment when there is absolutely no choice except to choose what is inevitable, I learned that in most of my life there is vast, vast choice.

I could not choose for Bonnie to live. I could not choose to avoid her death or sidestep it. I could not choose to keep her with me. I could not choose to feel no grief. But beyond that moment of her death, the path branched, turned, widened out into a vast landscape of choice.

I think this was the message my body or my subconscious was giving me on those occasions when I unaccountably came to a stop. I came to a stop when I was acting like a man without choice, acting as if all I could do was to plod forward. Then some instinct brought me to a stop, brought me to that moment of stillness from which every direction is equally possible.

When Carol came into my life, I followed my instincts— my instinct to trust my feelings for her, and my instinct that I needed to leave town. I went away to Michigan and I stayed away a month, in the way my instincts had told me to do. That month did what I thought it would do: It soothed me, it refreshed me. It rewarded me. It bathed me in love. It bathed me in my love for Bonnie; it bathed me in her love as I remembered it; it bathed me in the love of family and relatives and lifelong friends. It bathed me, too, through endless hours of phone conversations and e-mails and letters, in the love of a woman whom I had just met.

From where and to where does our path lead? My path led me out from the time of complete dedication to Bonnie's care and to our love; it led me out from the overwhelming sadness after her death. It led me out from a time when I did not, could not allow myself to feel all the sadness and permanence of her loss. The path has passed through deep sadness; it has passed through a time when I learned new ways of embracing my love for Bonnie; it has passed through a time when I embraced the love of a woman who came suddenly into my life. It has led me through an exploration and a discovery of my own power to create my life.

Where it's going I can't tell you, because I know now that life and circumstance may veto what I imagine, and I know now that I can create what I have not yet imagined. Between these two forces—the inevitable power of life to veto our plans and our own unfathomable power to create a future in every moment—lies the mystery of life, lies the possibility and the energy and the beauty of the world.

Head down, eyes locked,
Placing each labored step
ahead of the last
In a right line.
This is the way we walked
Through that rocky cleft,
This is the way, in grief,
we keep on walking
Focused on each narrow step
Through a spreading meadow
where we could run and play
If only we raised our face
To the wide horizon.

Letting Go of Grief

∶ TWO years after Bonnie died, I now spend far less time thinking about her than I did in that first year after she died. My life has changed vastly. I have married Carol and have three new stepchildren in my life. I'm opening the door to a new career and exploring, with Carol, avenues of personal growth that I knew nothing about, a year and a half ago.

My love for Bonnie is still with me, but no longer shows itself as intense grief. Sometimes it surfaces as waves of sadness, and that sadness often encompasses my mother and father, too, each of whom died within a year of Bonnie. Along with the sadness I feel about losing them is another regret—an unwillingness to let go of that sad and beautiful time of mourning when I was so intensely attuned to my love for each of them.

Sometimes, too, I experience a quiet feeling of guilt that I am not spending more time remembering Bonnie, as if I am abandoning her memory. Sometimes it feels disloyal not to hold on to every memory, every photograph, every way we did things together, every favorite recipe from our years together. Sometimes that tug of guilt is mixed with a worry that I may be still tucking my grief away in a place where it will be stuck, unexpressed and potentially destructive.

Perhaps what's going on is simply that both my life and my love for Bonnie are continuing to evolve. Each change in life brings a new grief for what is inevitably left behind. Morrie and Arleah Shechtman put it this way, in *Love in the Present Tense*: "A commitment to personal growth produces constant losses because each time you move forward to embrace the new, you have to let go of something old. The more you are awake and present in your life, the more you will feel these losses."

As hard as the first stunned months without Bonnie were, the newness of the tragedy created a time of sacred grief. When not having Bonnie became merely the day-to-day reality of my life, my grief at losing her was increased by the grief of losing that sacred intensity. Perhaps something like that is happening now: As I notice that my grief for Bonnie is no longer a day-to-day presence in my life, I feel a new sense of loss.

It's natural to hold on to grief. For months after Bonnie died, grief defined me. It gave me a sense of who I was when I felt that my life had been pulled out from under me. Then Carol came into my life, and I became part of a touching love story that included my grief, included the capacity for love that living in love with Bonnie had given me. My grief for Bonnie was still a daily presence in my life. Often Carol would hold me as I wept for Bonnie. Carol's love for me encompassed my love for Bonnie, and our love for each other had to encompass the sadness and the fear that I carried with me from losing Bonnie.

It's hard to leave that behind, hard to close a chapter of my life that was heartbreaking and passionate. Even now I can feel myself resisting giving up that story of grief and love. It's such a beautiful, sweet and sad tale. And, after all, people look to our stories for our identities. For a time, I was "Bonnie's canyon," the space left empty by her absence. Now, like all living things, I need to grow beyond what defined me in the past.

To let go of grief is to recognize that I'm outgrowing the story of Bonnie's death. That is different from outgrowing my love for her. To let go of grief is to recognize that my life is going on without her. That is death's doing, not mine.

To let go of grief is to recognize that her life does not need me. My memory of Bonnie's life is not her life. Her life is what it is, and nothing I do now will change one moment of it.

I may need what her life has given me—the values and ideals, the memory of her grace with people, the lessons learned about love. In order to be fully present to my life now, I may need to touch and open the places where I hold my sadness. But Bonnie does not need me.

The goodness and beauty of her life are not dependent

on what I remember or what I forget, and thus many of the imperatives that have shaped my life for these past two years dissolve. Yes, the memory of her life still holds indescribable beauty and inspiration. But it holds no obligations.

I can let go of grief.
That choice is up to me.
And when I do let go of grief,
I will grieve for that loss, too.
I learned to love Bonnie,
had to let her go.
I learned to love my grief,
and that, too, I must,
in the end,
let go.

An Ending That Is
No End

⁓ FOUR years, one month and three days after Bonnie died, I woke to a Norwegian violin piece that touched some deep sadness in me. Years had passed since those early days when grief would bring me to a standstill, forcing me to pause and pay attention; I noticed, though, that my work had been stalled for several days, as it had back then.

So I lit a candle and brought Bonnie's photo down from the fireplace mantel. I began to write a new ending to this book.

The end now is not the end that it was two years ago. In truth, there is no end to this book, just the place where I choose to stop for now. There isn't an end to my loving her and missing her—not before my own end. With the candle lit and her picture in front of me, my life with her (as well as her dying) seemed both distant and present, far in the past and as close as the sadness stirred up by the notes of a violin. Maybe what there is to say now, four years since I lost her, is not about grief, but about time.

We often speak of our past life, our lost loved ones, as if they are in some place that moves farther and farther from us with each passing year, like a town we've passed through on a train. We speak of "the distant past." This model of time—and it is just a model—has no room for the present pang of grief that is right now, right here.

Here's another image of time that's a better match for what I experience in grief: Rather than moving past the events of our life, we grow outward from them. Think how a tree grows—adding a layer around its circumference every year. The wood that was the sapling is still there, in the heartwood of the mature tree.

Seen from this viewpoint, the world occurs differently: Everything I was when Bonnie died is still here; my growth since then has not subtracted any of that, but added new layers of myself around the person I was then. This may not be a surprising viewpoint to introspective people who are keenly aware of the younger person who walks with them—within them. To the outside world, however, that younger person (you might say, all those younger people within us) exists only as stories about a time and a place that no longer exist.

For me, to say that Bonnie is now just a story from a

vanished past does not match my experience. It matches my experience of her absence, but not my experience of her continuing presence.

I seem better served by the model of time that places the past within me, like the sapling within the tree, rather than in a distant place to which I can never return. Viewing time through this model, I am not shocked at sadness rising suddenly, not surprised that the joy and the grief of loving Bonnie are still with me. It makes perfect sense to hear Carol say that she feels Bonnie's presence with us, though she and Bonnie never met.

I hold love and grief within me because they have shaped who I am. Perhaps it's easier to notice grief's abrupt wound than to discern the effects of love's gradual nurturing. But both give me who I am. Loving Bonnie and being loved by her have shaped what I hold as valuable and possible. Her love has shaped what I love and what I aspire to.

The model of "growing outward like a tree" accounts for what I find present in myself. In this model, I have grown outward from the happy and protected boy I was, outward from the serious teenager, outward from the young man who fumbled his first marriage, outward from the thirty-two-year-old man who fell in love with Bonnie, outward from the fifty-five-year-old man who held her as she died. These are layers in the core of my being.

The joy of loving Bonnie and the grief of losing her are available to me at any moment, because they are part of who I am. Bonnie is the place from which I grow. It would be senseless for me to pretend to grow *from* some other past, yet growing from that past imposes no limit on the direction in which I may choose to grow.

Within this view of time and growth, something else becomes clearly visible: the gift that Bonnie gave me.

The gift is not in anything she taught me, though she taught me countless things.

The gift is not that she loved me, though she did love me.

The gift is not that I loved her, though I loved her more than I had imagined I could love someone.

No, her gift to me is who I became in her presence, which is the origin of who I will ever become in her absence. Everything I will become flows through and from the man I was with her.

So, finally, her gift to me . . . is me.

In the face of such a gift, all I can do is all that any human being can do: to stand before the mystery of her existence and my own, with wonder.

With curiosity.

With gratitude.

With love.

If you would like to share your thoughts about
this book, or your own experiences of grief,
please visit www.lovinggrief.com.

GLOBAL *community*
INDIVIDUAL *awakening*

Larson Publications
larsonpublications.com

Larson Publications aspires to help bring forward a
new, creative universal outlook that embraces and transcends divisions
of east and west, north and south, believers and nonbelievers.